1900-1919

Richard Tames

Franklin Watts

London · New York · Sydney · Toronto

© Franklin Watts 1991

First published in Great Britain in 1991 by
Franklin Watts
96 Leonard Street
London EC2A 4RH

First published in the United States by
Franklin Watts Inc.
387 Park Avenue South
New York, N.Y. 10016

First published in Australia by
Franklin Watts
14 Mars Road
Lane Cove
NSW 2066

UK ISBN: 0 7496 0261 9

Design: K and Co
Editor: Hazel Poole
Picture Research: Ambreen Husain

Printed in Belgium

A CIP catalogue record for this book is available from the
British Library.

Photographs: Norman Barrett 32(B), 33(C); BFI Stills, Posters and Designs 37(TL),
37(TR); J. Chewter 20(CL); Coca Cola, Great Britain 43(BR) ("Coca Cola" and "Coke"
are registered trademarks of The Coca Cola Company); E.T. Archive 31(B); Mary
Evans Picture Library 21(T), 23(TL), 27(T), 27(BL), 30(BL), 30(T), 31(TL), 40(T),
41(TL), 41(TR), 42(T); Foreign and Commonwealth Office Library 17(BR); The
Hulton Picture Library 6(T), 6(BL), 7(TR), 7(BL), 7(BR), 9(BL), 9(BR), 10(T), 10(BL),
11(TR), 11(B), 12(T), 13(L), 14(T), 14(BL), 16(Both), 17(BL), 18(All), 19(Both),
20(CR), 20(B), 21(CL), 21(B), 23(TR), 24(T), 24(BR), 25(T), 25(CL), 25(B), 26(BL),
26(BR), 27(BR), 28(T), 28(B), 29(BL), 30(BR), 31(TR), 33(T), 33(B), 34(T), 35(TR),
36(T), 38(BR), 39(BL), 39(BR), 41(B), 44(L); Imperial War Museum 38(BL); Kobal
Collection 36(B), 37(BL); National Motor Museum 24(BL), 25(CR); Robert Opie 42(B);
Popperfoto 6(BR), 7(TL), 8(BL), 9(T), 10(BR), 11(TL), 13(R), 15(B), 17(T), 21(CR),
22(T), 22(B), 23(B), 26(T), 28(C), 29(T), 29(C), 29(BR), 32(T), 34(B), 35(TL), 35(B),
38(T), 39(TL), 40(B), 44(C), 44(R), 45(All); The Scout Association 43(T), 43(CL);
Topham 8(T), 8(BR), 14(BR), 15(T), 20(T); Visual Arts Library 39(TL).

Cover: Mary Evans Picture Library
Frontispiece: Mary Evans Picture Library

ROTHERHAM PUBLIC LIBRARIES

This book must be returned by the latest date entered above.
The loan may be extended [personally, by post or telephone]
for a further period if the book is not required by another reader.

LMI

Contents

FLIGHT SUB-LIEUT. R.A.J. WARNEFORD. V.C.

Introduction

Few English-speaking people who saw the dawn of the new century doubted that it would be one of peace, progress and prosperity. Looking back, it was clear that the years leading up to 1914 continued more or less the trends of previous decades. Then came "The Great War for Civilisation", which cut history in half, disrupting millions of ordinary lives, smashing major empires and re-drawing the world map.

At the British Foreign Office, when war was declared in 1914, Sir Edward Grey observed enigmatically "The lamps are going out all over Europe; we shall not see them lit again in our lifetime". The masses, on both sides, believed the war would be swift and cheap. They were to be swiftly but not cheaply disillusioned.

The drama of war obscured other changes, particularly in technology, which were to have a deep impact on the lives of nations and individuals. In 1900, motor vehicles were still seen as very expensive toys for the rich. By 1919, they were being mass-produced to revolutionise public and private transport.

In 1900, only dreamers took seriously the possibility of manned flight in heavier-than-air machines. In 1903, the Wright brothers proved it was not a dream. World War I made air forces a strategic weapon in their own right.

In 1919, two British aviators, Alcock and Brown, used a converted bomber to fly the Atlantic – 16 years after the Wright brothers' first epic flight which had only lasted 12 seconds. As statesmen assembled in Paris to construct a new world order out of the wreckage of the old, Alcock and Brown's brilliant feat could stand as a symbol that the bright hopes with which the century had dawned might not all prove to be illusions.

Britain in 1900-1919

In 1900, Britain was at war, struggling to defeat the armies of Boer farmers in South Africa. The unexpectedly high price of victory prompted changes of policy at home and abroad. The signing of the Anglo-Japanese alliance in 1902 enabled Britain to re-deploy more of her fleet in home waters. An entente with France in 1904 and with Russia in 1907 cleared up old disputes, but aligned Britain against the expanding power of Germany whose vigorous export trade and rapidly growing navy both seemed to threaten vital British interests.

The poor standards of health revealed by would-be recruits at the time of the Boer war helped the acceptance of a range of new welfare measures such as school medical inspections and free school meals, as well as the promotion of physical education in the interest of "national efficiency". Military reforms included the establishment of a general staff, the creation of cadet units at public schools and the founding of a Territorial Army of reservists. Some historians see the Edwardian era as the last golden glow of imperial greatness. Others see civil strife, gross inequality and a sluggish economy which drove one percent of the population to emigrate each year to countries which offered more hope and a chance to prosper.

△David Lloyd George in 1912. A brilliant peace-time reformer, he also proved to be an outstanding leader in war.

The labour movement grew rapidly with the founding of the Labour Party in 1900 and the organisation of large-scale industrial confrontations like the dock strike of 1911 (below left). Keir Hardie (below) was the first working man to enter Parliament.

◁Queen Victoria's death in 1901, after the longest reign in British history, marked the end of an era.

▽Edward VII looked every inch a king and thoroughly enjoyed playing the part.

◁HMS *Dreadnought*, launched in 1906.

▽Art students salute the relief of Mafeking.

Germany – Empire to Republic

As continental Europe's most populated and economically advanced country, Germany was bound to have a profound influence on its neighbours. German supremacy in music, philosophy and science was widely acknowledged and its pioneering schemes of social insurance were much applauded. Its brilliant achievements in technology, design and the arts were, however, overshadowed by the anxiety created by the expansion of its navy and the high profile of the military in the conduct of its national affairs.

German involvement in the politics of the Balkans and the Middle East caused further alarm. War, when it came, was scarcely unexpected. Germany was well prepared, both militarily and industrially but, failing to achieve the swift victory which had been planned, was eventually ground down by the superior resources of the Allies. The result was the utter discredit of the Kaiser's regime and the emergence, in disaster and defeat, of a democracy which never recovered from the dismal circumstances of its birth.

△ "Through our army, freedom of the seas". A war-time poster proclaims the challenge to British naval supremacy. (Left) The giant Krupp works at Essen – Germany's arsenal. (Below) Medical orderlies on parade. Germany was to suffer almost 2 million casualties in the course of World War I.

▷ "The supreme warlord" – Kaiser Wilhelm II at the military manoeuvres of 1910. Ambitious and impetuous, he refused to be restrained by the caution of his civilian advisers. After 1918, he fled to a long exile in neutral Holland.

▽ Political demonstrations in Berlin in 1919. The fall of the Kaiser's regime created a political vacuum which favoured the emergence of many left and right wing extremist groups. Violence on the streets was common and fed a widespread desire for a return to order and stability.

▷ A German warship awaiting demolition at Scapa Flow. Britain achieved at least one of its war aims in full – the destruction of the German High Seas Fleet, which had brought her to within six weeks of starvation through U-boat warfare.

Russia – from empire to revolution

In 1900, Russia was a vast multinational empire, less than half of which was Russian. Poles, Finns, Balts, Armenians, Jews and Muslims resented the official policies of "Russification", but found relative freedom in the inefficiency of the empire's sprawling bureaucracy. The disastrous Russo-Japanese war of 1904–5, and subsequent abortive revolution, forced the Tsar into a half-hearted experiment of ruling the country through a parliament (Duma). Disaster for the Romanov dynasty might, however, have been avoided had Russia not become entangled in World War I. Operations were conducted with staggering incompetence, provoking a liberal-led revolution which ousted the Tsar in order to fight the war more vigorously. Russia was, however, too weak to fight on and, in the chaos of disaster, a tiny minority of Bolshevik revolutionaries seized power and changed history.

△A rare photograph of the controversial "holy man", Gregory Efimovitch Rasputin. He bewitched the Russian aristocracy and exerted immense influence over the Tsar through his ability to control the effects of the Tsarevitch's haemophilia.

△The first Russian Duma (Parliament) in session in 1906. Russia had no tradition of government by consent and no effective method of co-operation between Tsar and Duma emerged.

▷Doomed – Tsar Nicholas II and his family. The Tsarina urged him not to give concessions to reformers who wanted to ward off a revolution. The whole family was killed on Lenin's orders in 1918.

△At the Finland Station! A romantic view of Lenin, as seen by communist artist Khvostenko, addressing soldiers and sailors on his arrival from exile in 1917. The Bolsheviks' ultimate success was based on their willingness to destroy all opposition. (Above right) One of the most spectacular events of the 1905 revolution was the mutiny of the battleship *Potemkin*, later immortalised in a film by the Soviet director Sergei Eisenstein. This picture shows Matsushenko, the alleged leader of the mutiny who is said to have killed 10 officers. Rather than surrender the ship, he wanted to blow it up!

▷Alexander Kerensky (left) became Minister of War in the 1917 Provisional Government. He was determined to maintain Russia's commitment to the fight but by the time he seized the levers of power, they were no longer connected to anything that worked. His brief career was followed by life-long exile.

End of empire – Austria-Hungary

In 1900, the Habsburg emperor, Franz-Jozef, ruled over a vast, shaky empire which stretched from the heart of Europe to the fringe of the Balkans. Power and privilege were virtually monopolised at the time by two nations which enjoyed special status – Austria and Hungary.

Vienna was the imperial capital but Budapest almost rivalled it in splendour, if not in size. Economic progress within the empire was very uneven, with islands of modern industry amid an ocean of peasant agriculture.

Cultural life, however, flourished. In Vienna, Sigmund Freud laid the foundations of psychoanalysis, while Lehar wrote light-hearted operas and Strauss composed dazzling waltzes. But even in the arts, new strains appeared as composers Smetana and Dvorak pioneered a fiercely nationalistic style of music among the Czechs.

The First World War broke the empire and its peoples seized a new future, while Austria was reduced to a small German-speaking republic.

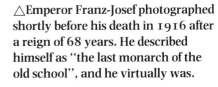

△Emperor Franz-Josef photographed shortly before his death in 1916 after a reign of 68 years. He described himself as "the last monarch of the old school", and he virtually was.

◁Early Polish postage stamps were hasty overprints of German stamps. This was symbolic of the chaos of the nation's re-birth. A modern stamp (top left) commemorates the hero turned dictator, Marshal Pilsudski.

 Tomas Masaryk, the founder-President of Czechoslovakia, was born the son of a coachman. He rose to become a Professor of Philosophy and an outspoken champion for the Czechs. In 1908, he exposed official skulduggery intended to discredit Croat nationalists. In 1914, he fled to London to plead the Czech cause and in 1917 raised a Czech Legion among prisoners of war in Russia. In 1918, he persuaded the United States to recognise the independence of his nation and returned home as its President-elect.

◁Bela Kun (far right), with fellow communist revolutionaries in August 1919, shortly after his fall from power. While serving with the Austro-Hungarian army during World War I, Kun was captured by the Russians and returned to his native Hungary as a communist agitator, provoking the fall of a weak liberal government. Throughout the summer, the communists ruthlessly pushed through radical reforms and made many enemies. Invaded by Czech and Rumanian forces, and faced with a counter-revolutionary movement under Admiral Miklos Horthy, Kun's regime disintegrated when Rumania entered Budapest. Kun fled, via Vienna, to Russia.

End of empire – Ottomans

By 1900, the sprawling Ottoman empire had lasted for six centuries but was under pressure from within and outside. Britain had taken control of Egypt and Cyprus, and France had control of Morocco. Italy was to seize Libya in 1911 and the small states of the Balkans to struggle for the empire's last European territories in 1912–13. The response of the Sultan's government was a policy of piecemeal modernisation to make its armed forces stronger and its administration more efficient.

These limited changes encouraged a dissident group of young Turks to revolt in 1908, force the sultan to abdicate and restore the short-lived democratic constitution of 1876. The new regime's decision to ally itself with Germany brought short-term benefits but was a strategic disaster in the long run. World War I proved a great strain on the empire's shaky structure and provoked major internal upheavals, including horrendous massacres of the Armenian community. With Germany's defeat came humiliating peace-terms and the dismemberment of the empire.

▽The Ottoman army was modernised to underpin the dynasty but ironically its officers were to take the lead in limiting the power of the Sultan. The army has continued to play a crucial role in Turkish politics ever since.

△Abd al-Hamid II accepted a democratic constitution on coming to power in 1876 but suspended it in 1878 and ruled as an absolute monarch until his deposition in 1909.

◁In 1915, the Allies tried to break the emerging deadlock on the Western Front by attacking the Gallipoli peninsula, with the aim of controlling the Dardanelles and thus a supply route to the Black Sea and Russia. "Johnny Turk" held the commanding heights bravely and the Allies, notably the newly-formed ANZAC troops from Australia and New Zealand, were pinned down on the beaches, where disease and combat took a terrible toll. The commander of the tough Turkish resistance was Mustafa Kemal who was to lead the post-war revolt which created a new Turkish republic. He became its first president.

The Ottoman empire was dynastic and multi-national. Its unity depended on the ability of its ruler to command loyalty or enforce obedience, rather than on any shared sense of national identity. Its ruling elite was mostly Turkish and Turks were a minority among the whole population. The British encouraged internal dissension among the tribes of the Arabian peninsula against their Ottoman overlords. The archaeologist T.E. Lawrence (right), a fluent Arabic speaker, proved himself a brilliant guerilla leader, and became a legend among Arabs and British alike. Although his "desert revolt" was only a sideshow to General Allenby's methodical conquest of Palestine, it did arouse a wish for independent statehood among the Arab peoples.

End of empire – China

China's half-hearted attempts to modernise came too late to save it from imperialist predators. In 1895, China was dramatically defeated by a rejuvenated Japan and lost Taiwan to the victor. In 1900, a widespread anti-foreign rising, led by a secret society of "Harmonious Fists" (hence the "Boxer" uprising), gained the support of the imperial court but petered out in bloody confusion. In 1911, a group of young Chinese, inspired by liberal political ideas of constitutional government, overthrew the Manchu dynasty. The provisional president of the infant Chinese republic, a western-educated doctor, Sun Yat-Sen, was obliged to give way to its leading general, Yuan Shih-Kai. Yuan died in 1916, having failed to establish a new dynasty, but having set a pattern for warlord rule which was to curse the country for an entire generation.

Meanwhile, Japan had taken advantage of World War I to seize German-held territories in China and to press for "Twenty One Demands" which aimed to reduce the country to the status of a satellite. In 1919, Peking students protested against Japanese aggression and this "May the Fourth" movement broadened into a more general demand for change, which resulted in a Chinese communist party in 1921.

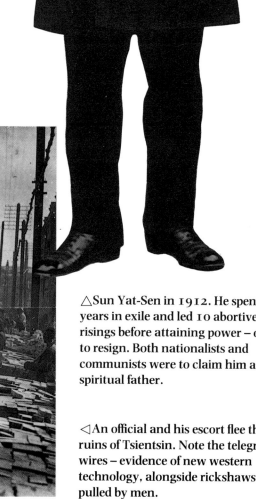

△Sun Yat-Sen in 1912. He spent 16 years in exile and led 10 abortive risings before attaining power – only to resign. Both nationalists and communists were to claim him as a spiritual father.

◁An official and his escort flee the ruins of Tsientsin. Note the telegraph wires – evidence of new western technology, alongside rickshaws pulled by men.

△Officers of the Manchu army
wearing western-style uniforms and
traditional pig-tails.

△Demonstrators carrying
the new Chinese
nationalist flag.

△ Foreign troops arrive to
crush the Boxer Rising

17

Birth of a nation – Ireland

The success of Irish Nationalists in forcing land reform in the 1880s encouraged them to press for "Home Rule". This provoked the creation of an Ulster Unionist party by Protestants determined to maintain the link with Britain. By 1914, both sides had built up private armies and civil war seemed imminent. The outbreak of World War I shelved the crisis and 200,000 Irishmen rushed to fight for Britain.

In April 1916, revolutionary Irish nationalists led by Patrick Pearse and James Connolly took advantage of British reverses in the war to launch an abortive "Easter Rising" in Dublin. It was crushed in days, but the execution of its leaders created martyrs and a myth to rally mass-support for total independence when the war ended. The 1918 election saw an overwhelming majority for Sinn Fein ("Ourselves Alone"), except in Ulster which remained solidly Unionist. The nationalists set up a Dail Eireann (Irish Parliament) and prepared for guerilla warfare.

▽This area of central Dublin was heavily shelled by a British gunboat during the Easter Rising in 1916.

△Sir Edward Carson, Unionist leader, addressing a Protestant rally in 1913. Their motto was "No Surrender".

△American-born Eamonn De Valera addressing a Los Angeles meeting in 1919. He later became Eire's president.

▷ A pro-British account of the Easter Rising stresses the sufferings of those caught in the crossfire. British troops were cheered as they put down the rebels, but the persecution which followed angered many. Although less than 1,000 people took part in the rising, over 2,500 were arrested and 1,867 imprisoned. Although 90 were condemned to death, only 15 were actually shot.

THE SINN FEIN RISING AS IT AFFECTED PEOPLE

The number of rebels killed at Dublin is not yet known, but over 3000 were captured. The civilians murdered by them total 160, including twenty women. The casualties among the troops are 124 killed, 388 wounded, and 9 missing. Seventeen officers were killed and 46 wounded.

THE SHOT REBELS: THOMAS MACDONAGH (POET), "MAJOR" MACBRIDE, EDWARD DALY, T. J. CLARKE AND JOSEPH PLUNKETT (POET)

FIREWOOD GATHERERS

The poor people have ransacked the ruins for firewood, and the disorganisation caused to the postal system by the

THE WIDOW'S LOAF

The rebels blow struck Ireland rather than England, for the poorest people have suffered acutely from lack of food, wh ch

THE IMPROVISED POST-BAG

estruction of the fine General Post Office where £30,000 in money was stolen—is ing met by all sorts of temporary devices.

THE REAL SUFFERERS: HUNGRY CHILDREN RECEIVING A DOLE OF BREAD

THE CHILDREN'S BITE

is now doled out by soldiers and priests. During the week-end following the rising nearly 100,000 persons received poor relief.

THE PRIEST AS PACIFIER

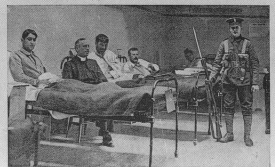

WOUNDED REBELS UNDER GUARD IN A TEMPORARY HOSPITAL AT THE CASTLE

REBELS UNDER GUARD

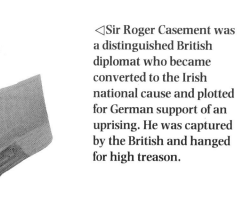

◁ Sir Roger Casement was a distinguished British diplomat who became converted to the Irish national cause and plotted for German support of an uprising. He was captured by the British and hanged for high treason.

World War I

World War I confounded the expectations of combatants on both sides who had expected that hostilities might be bloody but would also be short. In the end, it claimed the lives of over 10 million men with twice as many casualties.

Almost most of the combat took place in Europe, there were major campaigns in the Middle East and smaller ones from Africa to China, as well as naval engagements from the North Sea to the Falklands. Aerial warfare added a new dimension to the conflict and grew rapidly in importance as the war progressed.

The end, when it came, was sudden and unexpected. 1917 was a disastrous year for the Allies, with mutiny in the French army, an Italian collapse at Caporetto and Russia's dissolution into the turmoil of revolution. In the spring of 1918, Germany launched an offensive whose very success forced the Allies to co-ordinate their forces as never before and inflict a series of smashing counter-attacks to gain a decisive victory.

PRISONERS' RUSH FOR WATER

◁German prisoners of war – disillusioned by defeat, such men were to join Freikorps in Germany.
▽A file of weary British "Tommies" slog through a wasted countryside.

△Police arrest the Serbian assassins of Archduke Franz Ferdinand (top), heir to the Austrian throne, who was shot when he and his wife visited recently annexed Sarajevo.

▷ The British liner *Lusitania* was sunk in May 1915 by a German U-boat with the loss of 1,195 lives, 128 of whom were American citizens. The United States was outraged.

LEST WE FORGET

The Sinking of the Lusitania.
May 7th 1915.

FAC-SIMILE OF MEDAL STRUCK BY GERMANY
TO COMMEMORATE THE EVENT
Translation of wording on Medal
BUSINESS ABOVE EVERYTHING   NO CONTRABAND — THE
CUNARDLINE — CUNARD-BOOKING   GREAT LINER LUSITANIA

▽ Gas was first used by the Germans in April 1915, causing panic and many casualties among Allied troops. Primitive masks were rapidly developed. In the long run, however, the tank (below right), a British invention, proved more decisive in battle.

Votes for women

Nineteenth century reformers established women's rights to education, property and entry to professions, such as medicine. By 1900, the struggle for further emancipation had come to focus on the suffrage or vote. Once women could vote, it was believed that they would have the power to legislate away their other disabilities. The movement met fierce resistance and was divided over tactics.

The "suffragists" believed that only strictly legal methods, such as petitions and public meetings, should be used. To do otherwise would be to discredit the cause and prove that women were, indeed, too emotional to play a responsible part in public life. The "suffragettes", having tried constitutional means and found them futile, were willing to turn to direct action, though their attacks were on property, not people. The outbreak of war turned the energies of the campaigners into supporting the war effort, which they saw as an opportunity to prove women worthy of citizenship. They were right.

△Mrs Flora Drummond, known as "The General", is arrested at a demonstration in London's Hyde Park in 1914. On numerous occasions, police failed to intervene when suffragettes were attacked by counter-demonstrators.

◁Derby Day, 1913. Suffragette Emily Davidson dies from her injuries after throwing herself in front of King George V's horse. Her funeral became the occasion for a massive, dignified act of mourning. Her handbag was found to contain a return ticket to the racecourse, suggesting that she only intended to make the horse shy and not to seek martyrdom for the cause.

△Lady Astor, in front of a painting showing her as the first woman MP to take her seat in the House of Commons, addresses an audience of university women at the University of London's Bedford College.

△The "Cat and Mouse Act" allowed the release and re-arrest of imprisoned suffragettes who went on hunger-strike.

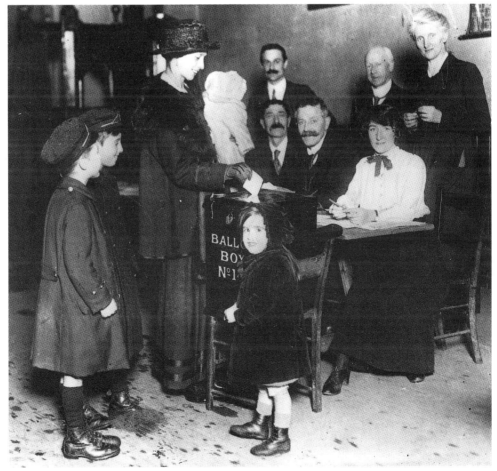

▷ At the general election of 1918, women over 30 were allowed to vote. In 1928, they got the vote at 21, the same as men.

23

The motor revolution

In Europe, the development of motor vehicles was initially driven by concern for their military potential, with Germany and France in keen rivalry. Britain was content to rely on foreign imports to provide what was, at first, seen as being an expensive toy for the rich. However, during the decade leading up to World War I, motor taxis and buses almost completely replaced horse-drawn vehicles in London for passengers.

In 1908, Henry Ford began production of his "Model T", the first cheap, reliable car for a mass-market. In 1913, he revolutionised the process of manufacture by introducing the moving assembly line, which enabled Ford workers to produce a car in 90 minutes.

World War I led to the placing of large government contracts for motor lorries and ambulances for army use. Many of these were later sold off as surplus after the conflict, to be bought by ex-soldiers who had learned to drive in the army and wanted to use their new skills in civilian life.

Thus the motor revolution moved on from passengers to freight, challenging at last, not the horse, but the railway itself.

△A showroom in London's fashionable West End advertises an imported American car. Note the emphasis given to its proven reliability. A Rolls Royce cost over six times as much as this.

▷George V being driven by the Honourable C.S. Rolls in an early Panhard. (Below) The Rolls Royce Silver Ghost could travel at over 60 mph. In 1907, the original model set a new reliability record of 14,371 miles without a breakdown.

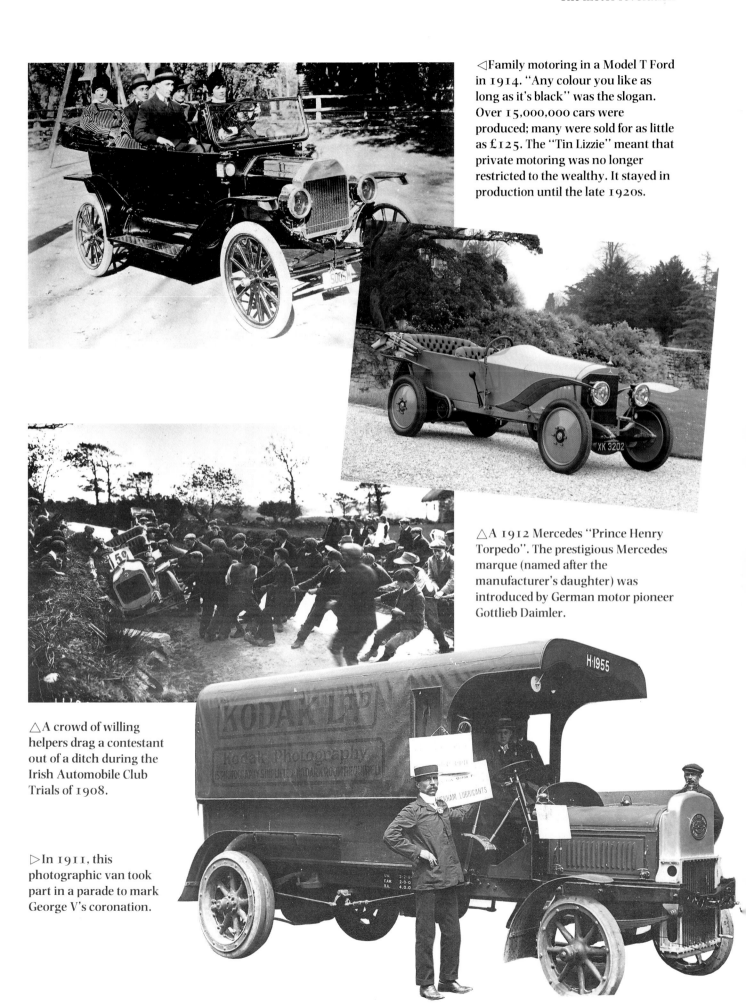

◁Family motoring in a Model T Ford in 1914. "Any colour you like as long as it's black" was the slogan. Over 15,000,000 cars were produced; many were sold for as little as £125. The "Tin Lizzie" meant that private motoring was no longer restricted to the wealthy. It stayed in production until the late 1920s.

△A 1912 Mercedes "Prince Henry Torpedo". The prestigious Mercedes marque (named after the manufacturer's daughter) was introduced by German motor pioneer Gottlieb Daimler.

△A crowd of willing helpers drag a contestant out of a ditch during the Irish Automobile Club Trials of 1908.

▷In 1911, this photographic van took part in a parade to mark George V's coronation.

Man flies!

Manned, powered flight was first achieved by Orville and Wilbur Wright on the flat sands at Kitty Hawk, North Carolina, on 17 December 1903. The distance covered, 36.5 metres, was less than the length of a modern jumbo jet. A new age had begun but the world was slow to grasp the achievement of the inspired amateurs who had financed their pioneering experiments from the profits of a small-town bicycle shop. The first published account of manned flight appeared in a bee-keeping journal!

Not until the Wright Brothers were managing flights of several miles and simple aerobatic manoeuvres did the significance of their breakthrough gain acceptance. Military applications were thought to be of the most immediate value and in 1908, the United States' Army became the first armed service in the world to acquire an "airforce".

In 1909, the Frenchman Louis Blériot flew across the English Channel in a plane of his own design. Rapid progress followed on both sides of the Atlantic. World War I accelerated this development even further, producing planes which were faster, larger, stronger and more reliable. The way was open for the birth of civil aviation as hostilities ended.

▽Wilbur (standing) sees Orville pilot the *Flyer* into history. (Left) Wilbur at the controls dressed in ordinary day clothes. Specialised flying gear was developed later to keep out the intense cold.

△This autographed invitation shows Alcock and Brown's transatlantic route from Newfoundland to Ireland. Their Vickers Vimy bomber took 16 hours 27 minutes to complete the flight.

◁First flight of the Zeppelin airship at Lake Constance in 1900. This revolutionary ship, designed by former Germany Army Officer Count von Zeppelin, used lightweight aluminium and a petrol engine. Commercial airship services using Zeppelins began in 1910. During World War I they were used to bomb Britain.

◁A fanciful view of Louis Blériot landing near Dover Castle after his 37 minute flight from Calais 23 miles away. In fact, his landing was anything but smooth and damaged his plane considerably.

△German air ace Baron von Richthofen (left), the "Red Baron", shot down over 80 planes before being shot down himself by a Canadian pilot and Australian ground-fire in 1918.

Science and medicine

To most people, the great advances in science and medicine made in the first two decades of the 20th century were quite literally invisible. This is because they involved the understanding or application of forces or substances which could not be detected with the naked eye. Radio seemed to be most immediately useful, although its applications were seen to be limited to controlling the movements of armies or of ships at sea. It was not until after World War I that it was thought of as a possible medium for entertainment.

The significance of the emerging discipline of nuclear physics, concerned with fathoming the structure of matter at the level of the atom and the universe, was far less readily grasped, even by the educated. In Germany, and to a lesser extent in America, politicians and opinion leaders had a growing respect for science. But in Britain, there was no attempt to draw up an official science policy until 1916.

◁ The sensational arrest of Dr Crippen aboard a liner in 1910 – the first murderer to be caught in flight by means of radio. (Below) Guglielmo Marconi, the Italian inventor of "wireless telegraphy".

△ The three scientific papers published by Albert Einstein at the age of 26 revolutionised physics. In 1916, he published his *General Theory of Relativity* and went on to win the Nobel Prize for Physics in 1921.

◁Pierre and Marie Curie, discoverers of two new elements, radium and polonium, shared the Nobel Prize for Physics in 1903. After Pierre's death in 1906, Marie succeeded him as a professor of physics at the University of Paris. In 1911, she was awarded the Nobel Prize for Chemistry. During World War I, she set up an X-ray service, saving thousands of lives.

▷ The career of (Lord) Ernest Rutherford illustrated the growing internationalisation of science. Born in New Zealand, he is pictured here at McGill University in Canada. He went on to head the world-famous Cavendish Laboratory in Cambridge. He won the 1908 Nobel Prize for Chemistry and developed the nuclear theory of atomic structure.

◁Robert Koch, discoverer of the bacilli which cause cholera, anthrax and tuberculosis, won the 1905 Nobel Prize for Medicine.

△Thomas Edison, the last of the self-taught inventors, seen here with the phonograph, one of his 1,300 patents.

Music and dance

Music in popular culture was changed forever by the development of recording and broadcasting. A patent on recording cylinders was granted in the United States in 1900. The 78 rpm phonograph record, which was to oust the cylinder, appeared the following year. By 1902, recording attracted the talents of world-famous Italian tenor Enrico Caruso.

The first music radio broadcast took place in Austria in 1904, and in 1905 the jukebox made its first appearance in the United States. America set trends for musical taste throughout the affluent world. The full impact of these new marvels would not, however, be felt until the 1920s.

Most people still had to make their own music or rely on the skills of those who could. Many work-groups and churches supported choirs or brass bands, and a piano was regarded as a highly desirable status symbol for the home.

There was, therefore, an immense demand for sheet music. In 1910, annual sales in the United States exceeded 200 million copies and in 1918 the sentimental ballad *Till We Meet Again* sold $3\frac{1}{2}$ million copies in a few months.

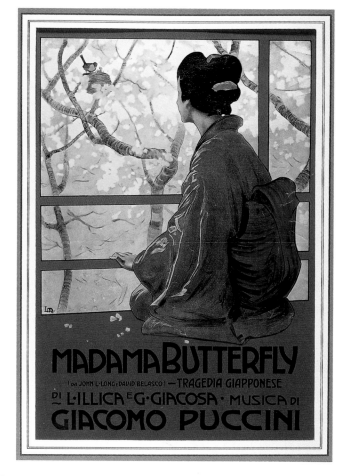

◁Recordings made Enrico Caruso known to millions who otherwise would never have heard him in one of his 50 opera roles.

△Puccini dominated opera with *Madama Butterfly* (1904). Russian dancer Anna Pavlova (below) formed her own ballet company.

△The unconventional dancing of Isadora Duncan shocked her native America but was applauded in Europe where she made a profound impact on dance education.

△The "Cakewalk" was one of many popular dance crazes to invade Europe from America. Like the "Turkey Trot" and "Grizzly Bear", it was intended to amuse the young, shock the old and be as different as possible from the formal elegance of the waltz.

▷Dancer/choreographer Vaslav Nijinsky was the star of the famed Ballets Russes established in Paris in 1909 by impresario Sergei Diaghilev, whose lavish productions revolutionised ballet and attracted such talents as stage designers Picasso and Matisse and composers Debussy and Ravel. Nijinsky created the role of Petrouchka, but his career ended in 1919 with the onset of madness.

COMOEDIA

4ᵐᵉ Année N° 16
15 Mai 1912
Numéro Exceptionnel
60 Pages
PRIX
1 fr. 50

7ᵐᵉ Saison
des
Ballets
Russes

NIJINSKI, dans l'"Après-Midi d'un Faune"
Aquarelle originale de Léon Bakst.

Sport

Numerous factors combined to increase the importance of sport in the first two decades of the 20th century – the revival of the ancient Greek ideal of an Olympic Games by Baron de Coubertin in 1896; the intensification of national rivalries which led up to World War I; the influence throughout the Empire and among the English-speaking peoples of British public school belief in the "character-building" value of competitive games; the concern to combat the harmful effects of bad living and working conditions of the growing populations in great industrial cities; the demand of potential spectators at all social levels for contests to fill their leisure hours; and the willingness and ability of cheap mass-circulation papers to provide coverage of such conveniently predictable events.

The international influence of Britain, which had laid down the rules of most sports from boxing to horse-racing, was supreme. The Wimbledon Lawn Tennis and Croquet Club and the Marylebone Cricket Club may have taken their names from London districts, but they were in effect, the world governing bodies for their respective sports.

△American Jim Thorpe won gold medals for the pentathlon and decathlon at the 1912 Stockholm Olympics, but was stripped of them when it was learned that he had once played baseball professionally.
◁Sensation at the 1908 Olympics as exhausted Italian Dorando Pietri crosses the line first, but loses the medal because officials helped him. He was given a special gold cup in consolation.

▷May Sutton and Mrs Hillyard (right) as doubles partners. Mrs Hillyard was six times Wimbledon champion. In 1905, May Sutton became the first American to win the title and won again in 1907. Wimbledon became an international competition from 1901 onwards. In 1907, every title "went abroad". A 1913 contest between New Zealander Tony Wilding and American Maurice McLoughlin drove Centre Court ticket prices to an unheard of £10! In 1914, the Centre Court was extended to take an extra 1,200 spectators. Wimbledon was, however, suspended from 1915 to 1918 because of World War I.

◁Jack Dempsey knocks out 35-year-old Jess Willard in 1919 to become heavyweight champion of the world. When he later retired, he became a successful New York restaurant owner. For many poor boys, boxing offered one of the few avenues to real wealth, but a career like Dempsey's was the exception, not the rule.

▷A Danish gymnastic team demonstrating at the White City stadium in 1908. Scandinavia led the way in the scientific development of physical training and "Swedish drill" was adopted in British schools during this period as a contribution to "national efficiency". Sport was increasingly appreciated as capable of making a positive contribution to the community.

Hitting the headlines

By 1900, the newspaper was a 200-year-old invention – and just beginning to reach a mass-readership. Compulsory education was creating something quite new in history – entire populations that were literate. The United States was one of the first countries to achieve mass literacy. As a democracy, it valued the education of its citizens, however basic that level may be.

American editors developed new attention-grabbing techniques, such as bold headlines, dramatic pictures and a terse, easy-to-read style. Other countries began to imitate these methods of boosting circulation. An American journalist of the period defined news as "whatever makes a reader say 'Gee Whizz!'", so newspapers concentrated on reporting the real dramas of wars and natural disasters and the artificial dramas of sport and the social life of the rich and the famous.

World War I provided an ultimate source and standard of dramatic stories, eclipsing virtually every other news story. With the existence of nations at stake, the global conflict turned newspapers from an indulgence to a necessity, turning occasional readers into news addicts. Ironically, what should have been a force for enlightenment became a tool of propaganda as both sides controlled the press to sustain popular commitment to the war.

◁The luxury liner represented the ultimate means of travel in terms of speed and comfort. The White Star liner *Titanic* was pronounced "unsinkable" at its launch. On its maiden voyage it struck an iceberg in mid-Atlantic and sank within minutes. There were too few lifeboats to take its 2,224 passengers and over 1,500 people died.

▽In 1911, the American explorer Hiram Bingham stumbled on the ruins of Macchu-Picchu, a vast mountain stronghold of the Inca empire, unknown to the outside world for four centuries until its re-discovery.

RUINS OF THE CITY AFTER EARTHQUAKE AND FIRE
SAN FRANCISCO. CAL.

△San Francisco after the earthquake and fire of 1906. Other disasters of the time included the eruptions of Vesuvius (1906) and Mont Pelee (1902).

▽Captain Robert Scott (centre) with his expedition party at the South Pole in 1912. They found Roald Amundsen's Norwegian flag already there. All of the party died on the way home.

Birth of the movies

In the 1890s, inventors in Europe and America patented over 100 different types of film camera and projector in the race to make "moving photography". The American Thomas Edison's first film was less than a minute long and showed one of his assistants sneezing. His films were the first on the commercial market, but had to be viewed through a peep-show machine. He thought films projected on a screen would be seen by too many people at once to make any money. This left the way clear for the French Lumière brothers to develop projected films for mass audiences.

Another French pioneer, Georges Méliès, was the first to see the possibilities of trick-photography, which he used in his fantasy *Voyage to the Moon* (1902). Progress was rapid. American Edwin Porter's 12-minute *The Great Train Robbery* (1903) was shot on outside locations and ended with a sudden close-up of a gunman firing straight at the audience. By 1910, there were almost 5,000 cinemas in Britain alone, but it was not until the 1920s that moving pictures were matched with recorded sound.

△Charlie Chaplin was the first motion picture "superstar". In 1913, he went to California and worked for the Keystone Company where he invented his famous baggy-trousered tramp character. He was a superb athlete and master of timing and gesture, much loved by World War I troops.

◁The spectacular set of D.W. Griffith's *Intolerance* (1916), a complex moralistic epic set in different historical periods, involved massive expense and a huge cast of extras. After the Russian revolutionary Lenin saw this film he declared that cinema would become "the foremost cultural weapon of the proletariat".

◁Theda Bara – prototype of a new film phenomenon, the star created by publicity. Her real name was Theodosia Goodman; her stage name was an anagram of "Arab Death". It was claimed that she was the daughter of a French artist and an Arabian princess, although this was inaccurate. She appeared in over 40 silent films including *Carmen* (1915) and *Cleopatra* (1917).

◁A typically crowded scene from D.W. Griffith's saga of the American Civil War, *Birth of a Nation* (1914). Its sympathy for the Confederate point of view angered many but in doing so made cinema an art-form for serious discussion.

△David Wark Griffith raised the silent cinema from the level of a fairground amusement to a serious form of art and the basis of a major branch of the entertainment industry. He was one of the earliest film-makers to work in California and built up a brilliant team of players including Mary Pickford, Lillian Gish and Lionel Barrymore.

The arts

Developments in the arts were contrary. More people than ever before had the money, leisure and education to enjoy literature, music and art. Yet artists seemed less and less concerned about communicating with ordinary people. The advent of photography drove painters and sculptors to represent likeness through experimental techniques which could convey what they believed the camera could not – subtleties of light, mood and movement.

Literature perhaps stayed closer to popular taste than art or even the avant-garde music of a composer like Schoenberg. But even popular writers seemed to comment on contemporary society in order to criticise its materialism and injustice.

Whereas the role of the artist had once been to celebrate the achievements of a people, it seemed that the painter or poet was someone who deliberately chose to live apart, uncomprehending of ordinary people and hard for them to understand.

△In 1907, Rudyard Kipling became the first English writer to win the Nobel Prize.

◁ *Troops Resting*, by C.R.W. Nevinson, Red Cross volunteer and war artist. Poet Wilfred Owen (below) was killed a week before the war ended.

▷ Picasso's "Harlequin". Painted in 1918 – it definitely doesn't look like a photograph!

△Avant-garde Spanish artist Pablo Picasso in front of a poster for Diaghilev's Russian ballet, for which he designed scenery and costumes.

◁American novelist Upton Sinclair fought social injustice in over 80 books.

▽Jack London rose from poverty to become America's most popular writer.

Fashion

The invention of the sewing machine and the mass-production of military uniforms laid the foundations of the modern fashion industry in the mid-nineteenth century.

By 1900, a wide range of garments could be bought "off the peg", though it was still common for the customer to have a garment slightly altered to fit exactly.

In progressive circles, "dress reformers" promoted the view that clothes should follow the line of the human body rather than distort it with corsets, padding or elaborate decoration. The growing popularity of sport and belief in the value of exercise assisted the trend towards lighter, looser garments. The modern woman's suit, consisting of tailored jacket and skirt, evolved from formal riding clothes.

At the same time that women's outerwear became less fussy, glamorous crepe de chine lingerie began to replace the severely plain underwear of the past.

Men's clothing, by contrast, changed more slowly, although a "military" look was favoured during wartime.

△Fashions for the year 1902. Note the S-shaped figure and pinched waist. Skirts reached right to the ground which made them impractical for outdoor wear. Note how high-necked the costumes are. Evening wear, by contrast, often revealed the shoulders. The wealthy wore different clothes according to the time of day.

◁Wealthy city-dwellers were dressing in much the same way throughout Europe and the Americas. In Asia, only the Japanese were beginning to dress like this family in Mexico City. Note that everyone wears a hat and that the ladies have long gloves. Lace was much used for decoration, although it was difficult to clean.

△Tennis was growing in popularity. The need for freedom of movement meant looser, lighter clothes. Note how this costume is trimmed in blue and white – a tribute to national pride in the navy.

▽Outdoor fashions for 1913. Note the contrasts with those of 1902 opposite – the whole line is softer and more flowing, shoes and necks are revealed. The hats, though still large, are less rigid and softened by feathers. Parasols were seen as an essential fashion accessory.

◁The *Tailor and Cutter* magazine of 1902 shows a full range of dress for the upper class male. Only the model with the informal smoking jacket (third from right, top) does not have a hat – and even he is carrying one. Note the long, heavy coat and flat hat (first left, bottom row) designed for motoring. Cars were open to the wind and rain and therefore very cold!

Growing up

One of the best things about growing up at the beginning of the 20th century was that children were increasingly likely to do so! Infant mortality rates fell rapidly as a result of improved diets and hygiene, better medical care and clean water supplies even in the poorest slums. "Summer diarrhoea", which had killed thousands of infants each year through intestinal infections, gradually became a thing of the past, though measles and scarlet fever could still be fatal.

Educational opportunities increased, though in Britain only one child in eight received full-time schooling after the age of 14, and half were working at least part of the time from the age of 12.

Youngsters were treated to new toys, such as the Teddy bear and Meccano sets. They could join the Boy Scouts or the Girl Guides. Children's literature flourished with the publication of L. Frank Baum's *The Wonderful Wizard of Oz* (1900), Beatrix Potter's *Peter Rabbit* (1902) and Kenneth Grahame's *The Wind in the Willows* (1908). The new century brought new ways to have fun.

△J.M. Barrie's *Peter Pan*, or *The Boy Who Wouldn't Grow Up* was an immediate success. A statue of Peter Pan was erected in Kensington Gardens opposite Barrie's house – overnight, as if by magic! Barrie bequeathed the valuable royalties from the play to the Great Ormond Street Hospital for Sick Children.

◁ *Meccano*, a constructional toy, was an indirect tribute to Anglo-American triumphs in engineering.

△ The Boy Scout movement was founded in 1908 by Robert Baden-Powell, a hero of the Boer War, to provide a healthy and patriotic outlet for young men. The Scouts soon eclipsed the church-based Boys' Brigade and inspired the formation of a parallel organisation, Girl Guides. Within a few years, Scout Troops could be found in 50 countries.

▷ Coca Cola first came to Britain from America in 1900.

43

Personalities 1900-1919

Asquith, Herbert Henry (1852–1928), Liberal Prime Minister between 1908–16. Intelligent and easy-going, Asquith presided successfully over a brilliant reforming administration, but was ousted from the wartime premiership in favour of the energetic Lloyd George.

Balfour, Arthur James (1848–1930), Conservative Prime Minister of Britain 1902–6. His diplomatic skill later made him Foreign Secretary (1916–19) and a leading figure at the Paris Peace Conference, as well as chief British representative at the League of Nations. He regarded the "Balfour Declaration" (1917) as his most important achievement.

Bethmann-Hollweg, Theobald von (1856–1921), German Chancellor 1909–17. Lacking experience in foreign affairs, Bethmann was pressurised into war by the armed services, which finally forced him out of office over his opposition to unlimited U-boat warfare. As he had feared, that policy brought America into the war.

Burns, John (1858–1943), the first British working man to enter the Cabinet. A powerful mob orator, he was committed to temperance, trade unionism and pacifism. He resigned from the government and public life on the outbreak of World War I.

Campbell-Bannerman, Henry (1836–1908), Liberal Prime Minister 1905–8. The first British politician ever to hold the official title of Prime Minister, he proved a popular leader too ill to reap the rewards of his ability, dying three weeks after his resignation.

Chamberlain, Joseph (1836–1914), Liberal politician who revolutionised the administration of Britain's second city, Birmingham, by pioneering social reforms. His efforts to protect British industry by campaigning for "Tariff Reform" embarrassed the government.

Clemenceau, Georges (1841–1929), Prime Minister of France 1906–09 and 1917–20.

D'Annunzio, Gabriele (1863–1938), Italian writer and adventurer. Author of sensational novels, pioneering aviator and war hero, D'Annunzio led the seizure of the disputed city of Fiume (1919) before retiring into private life. He was chiefly responsible for reviving the Roman open-arm salute adopted by Fascists and Nazis.

Diaz, Porfirio (1830–1915), Mexican general and dictator. A radical turned reactionary, Diaz ran an efficient administration (1876–1910) which benefited foreign investors and oppressed the peasant majority.

Ferdinand I (1861–1948), King of Bulgaria from 1887 to 1918. The "Fox of the Balkans" made Bulgaria totally independent of the Ottoman empire in 1908, but chose the wrong side in the general Balkan assault on the Ottomans in 1912 and World War I. When his troops mutinied, he abdicated in favour of his son, Boris, in 1918.

Ford, Henry (1863–1947), American industrialist who perfected the assembly-line technique to produce the world's first cheap, mass-produced car. As an employer he was both enlightened and authoritarian, paying good wages and fighting unions.

Grey, Sir Edward (1862–1933), British Foreign Secretary 1905–16, who influenced Britain's decision to enter World War I.

Kerensky, Alexander (1881–1970), Russian politician who was catapulted to supreme authority in the chaos of 1917. His vigorous efforts to stay in the war led to an abrupt fall from power and exile for the rest of his life.

Lloyd George, David (1863–1945), British Prime Minister 1916–22. A superb orator, energetic reformer and skilled negotiator, the "Welsh Wizard" was responsible for major welfare changes as Chancellor of the Exchequer 1908–15 and for

Herbert Asquith

Arthur Balfour

Henry Ford

invigorating the conduct of the war as the first Minister of Munitions 1915–16. He became Prime Minister in 1916.

Luxemburg, Rosa (1871–1919), German revolutionary socialist. Polish-born and Swiss-educated, Rosa Luxemburg worked tirelessly to unite revolutionary socialists across national boundaries. Her militant opposition to war led to her imprisonment by the German government and her involvement in an abortive revolution led to death at the hands of right-wing Freikorps.

Massey, William Ferguson (1856–1925), Prime Minister of New Zealand from 1912 to 1925. Massey was an enthusiastic supporter of Imperial co-operation in war and peace.

Milner, Alfred (1854–1925), British imperial statesman. Anglo-German by birth, he served with distinction in South Africa from 1897 to 1906 and was an influential member of Lloyd George's coalition government.

Northcliffe, Lord Alfred Harmsworth (1865–1922), British pioneer of popular journalism who launched the *Daily Mail* in 1896 and the *Daily Mirror* in 1903. He also owned the *Observer* and *The Times*. He financed lavish publicity stunts and advised on propaganda during World War I.

Pankhurst, Emmeline (1858–1928), British pioneer of women's suffrage. Having founded the Women's Social and Political Union, Mrs Pankhurst adopted militant tactics and was repeatedly imprisoned until turning her energies towards supporting the war effort. The granting of rights to women led to her departure from the Independent Labour Party and from Britain. Her daughters Christabel, Sylvia and Adela were all active feminists.

Pilsudski, Jozef (1867–1935), Polish statesman. A socialist agitator and nationalist revolutionary, he raised and led a Polish legion during World War I and was made head of state of newly-independent Poland in 1918. He ruled Poland as virtual dictator from 1926 to 1935.

Roosevelt, Theodore (1858–1919), President of the United States from 1901 to 1909. A dynamic character, "Teddy" Roosevelt was a cowboy turned soldier who became a crusading politician and died an explorer. An informed internationalist, he was the first head of state to win the Nobel Peace Prize in 1906, and was an early pioneer of environmental conservation.

Scott, Captain Robert Falcon (1868–1912), British explorer. A career naval officer, he led three major expeditions to the Antarctic, dying on his return from the South

Pole. His dogged courage won him a posthumous knighthood.

Smuts, Jan Christiaan (1870–1950), South African statesman. Having commanded Boer forces against the British, he worked actively for reconciliation after the war and led Union forces against the German African colonies in 1915–16. An influential member of the Imperial War Cabinet (1917–24) and Paris Peace Conference, he served as premier of South Africa between 1919 and 1924, before graduating to the status of a world statesman.

Taylor, F.W. (1856–1915), American industrial engineer. His innovative "time and motion" studies became the basis of a new approach to industry, summarised in his *Principles of Scientific Management* (1911), and used by manufacturers like Henry Ford.

Togo, Heihachiro (1846–1934), Japanese admiral. British-trained commander of the Japanese navy which annihilated the Russian fleet at the battle of Tsushima in 1905.

Witte, Count Sergei Yulievich (1849–1915), Russian statesman. A hard-working administrator who created the Trans-Siberian railway, Witte was recalled to serve briefly as Russia's first Prime Minister (1905–6). His warnings of revolution were ignored.

David Lloyd George

Emmeline Pankhurst

Jan Christiaan Smuts

1900-1919 year by year

1900

- Anti-foreign Boxer Rising in China.
- First Davis Cup contest – America beats Britain at tennis.
- Paper clip patented.
- First off-shore oil-well drilled.
- Olympic Games and World Exhibition held in Paris.
- British Labour Party founded.
- Major famine in India.
- Siege of Mafeking relieved in South African (Boer) War.
- Assassination of Italian King Umberto I.
- Deaths of critic John Ruskin, composer Sir Arthur Sullivan and dramatist Oscar Wilde.

1901

- Commonwealth of Australia established.
- First multi-storey car park.
- Death of Queen Victoria.
- Safety razor invented.
- First Nobel Prizes awarded.
- First transatlantic radio transmission.
- U.S. troops crush nationalist revolt in the Philippines.
- U.S. President William McKinley assassinated; Theodore Roosevelt becomes President.
- Deaths of composer Giuseppe Verdi and artist Henri Toulouse-Lautrec.

1902

- Treaty of Vereeniging ends South African (Boer) war.
- Establishment of Sinn Fein ("Ourselves Alone") as Irish republican party.
- Beatrix Potter's *Peter Rabbit* is published.
- Deaths of diamond millionaire Cecil Rhodes and novelist Emile Zola.

1903

- Ford Motor Company founded.
- First Tour de France bicycle race held.
- Women's Social and Political Union founded to fight for the vote for women.
- Wright Brothers fly first heavier-than-air plane.
- Assassination of King and Queen of Serbia.
- Deaths of painters Gauguin, Whistler and Pissarro.

1904

- "Entente Cordiale" signed between Britain and France.
- Outbreak of Russo-Japanese war.
- British expedition reaches Tibet.
- Olympic Games held in St. Louis in the United States.
- Deaths of explorer Sir Henry Stanley, composer Dvorak and writer Chekhov.

1905

- Norway becomes independent of Sweden.
- Treaty of Portsmouth ends Russo-Japanese war.
- Deaths of writer Jules Verne and actor Sir Henry Irving.

1906

- HMS *Dreadnought* launched.
- Eruption of Mount Vesuvius.
- Earthquake devastates San Francisco.
- Russia's first elected parliament (Duma) opens.
- Deaths of dramatist Ibsen and painter Cezanne.

1907

- Gandhi leads civil disobedience campaign in South Africa.
- First Boy Scout camp held at Brownsea Island, Dorset.
- First celebration of Mother's Day.
- Deaths of composer Edvard Grieg and scientist Lord Kelvin.

1908

- Young Turks' revolt limits power of Ottoman Sultan Abdul Hamid II.
- Austria-Hungary annexes provinces of Bosnia and Herzegovina.
- Olympic Games and Franco-British Exhibition held in London.
- Earthquake destroys Messina, Sicily killing 200,000.
- Death of composer Rimsky-Korsakov.

1909

- National Association for the Advancement of Coloured People established in America.
- Louis Blériot flies the English Channel.
- Old Age Pensions introduced in Britain.
- American Commander Robert Peary reaches the North Pole.
- Deaths of poet A.C. Swinburne and dramatist J.M. Synge.

1910

- Union of South Africa established.
- Major constitutional crisis in Britain.
- Japan annexes Korea.
- Revolution overthrows Portuguese monarchy.

- Girl Guides established.
- Radon discovered.
- Deaths of Edward VII, nursing pioneer Florence Nightingale, writers Mark Twain, O. Henry and Tolstoy and painter Holman Hunt.

1911

- "Agadir crisis" brings France and Germany to the brink of war.
- Manchu dynasty overthrown in China and a republic established.
- George V receives homage of the Indian princes at "Delhi Durbar".
- Parliament Act resolves constitutional crisis in the United Kingdom.
- Italy annexes Libya.
- Major strikes in Britain.
- Amundsen beats Scott to the South Pole.
- Assassination of Russian premier Stolypin.
- Deaths of composer Mahler and writer/librettist W.S. Gilbert.

1912

- Balkan states attack Ottoman empire.
- Sinking of the *Titanic*.
- Albania declares its independance.
- First use of zips in clothing.
- Olympic Games held in Stockholm.
- Death of novelist August Strindberg.

1913

- Panama Canal completed.
- Ford Motor Company introduces moving assembly line.
- First Chelsea Flower Show.
- Assassination of Mexican President Madero and King George I of Greece.
- Deaths of explorer Captain Scott and of inventor Rudolf Diesel.

1914

- Ireland on the brink of civil war.
- Outbreak of World War I.
- Anglo-French forces halt German advance at Battle of the Marne.
- Russian armies destroyed at the Battle of Tannenberg.
- Panama Canal opens.

1915

- First use of poison gas in warfare.
- Liner *Lusitania* sunk by German U-boat.
- ANZAC forces attempt landings at Gallipoli peninsula in Turkey.
- Nurse Edith Cavell shot by Germans.
- Death of poet Rupert Brooke.

1916

- Battle of Jutland – major naval engagement of World War I.
- Battle of the Somme.
- Battle of Verdun.
- First use of tanks in war.
- Abortive "Easter Rising" in Dublin.
- Arab revolt against Ottoman rule.
- Lord Kitchener drowned at sea.
- Wolf Cubs established.
- Albert Einstein proposes *General Theory of Relativity*.
- Deaths of writers Henry James and Jack London.

1917

- The United States enters World War I.
- Revolution in Russia forces Tsar's abdication.
- Finland proclaims independence.
- Allenby captures Jerusalem.
- Balfour Declaration commits British government to support a "Jewish national home in Palestine".

- Deaths of showman "Buffalo Bill" Cody, painter Edgar Degas and sculptor Auguste Rodin.

1918

- Treaty of Brest-Litovsk ends war between Bolshevik Russia and Central Powers.
- Civil war in Russia leads to murder of Tsar and his family.
- President Woodrow Wilson proposes Fourteen Points, a plan for world peace.
- Austria becomes a Republic.
- T.E. Lawrence leads Arabs into Damascus.
- Germany accepts terms of Allied armistice.
- Death of composer Claude Debussy.

1919

- Communist rising crushed in Germany.
- Treaty of Versailles signed in Paris.
- Amritsar massacre – British forces kill unarmed Indian demonstrators.
- First airline links established between London and Paris.
- Alcock and Brown fly the Atlantic non-stop.
- Fascist Party established in Italy.
- Paris Peace Conference redraws European frontiers.
- Worldwide influenza epidemic.

Index